Real-Life Heroes

By James Buckley Jr.

US Senior Editor Shannon Beatty
Senior Editor Caryn Jenner
Assistant Editor Kritika Gupta
Art Editors Emma Hobson, Roohi Rais
Jacket Editor Francesca Young
Jacket Designers Dheeraj Arora, Amy Keast
DTP Designers Mohd. Rizwan, Dheeraj Singh
Senior Cartographer Subhashree Bharati
Senior Picture Researcher Sumedha Chopra
Producer, Pre-Production Dragana Puvacic
Producer Niamh Tierney
Deputy Managing Editor Vineetha Mokkil
Managing Editor Laura Gilbert
Managing Art Editors Neha Ahuja Chowdhry, Diane Peyton Jones
Art Director Martin Wilson
Publisher Sarah Larter

Reading Consultant
Linda Gambrell, Ph.D.

First American Edition, 2017
Published in the United States by DK Publishing
345 Hudson Street, New York, New York 10014

The publisher would also like to thank the following for their kind permission to reproduce their photographs:
(Key: a=above, b=below/bottom, c=center, l=left, r=right, t=top)

1 Dreamstime.com: Digitalstormcinema. **3 NASA:** ESA (crb). **4-5 iStockphoto.com:** usas (b). **6 Alamy Stock Photo:** Mirko Seifert / dpa picture alliance (cr). **Ishwor Ghimire:** Pradeep Nepali (bl). **7 Alamy Stock Photo:** David Warren (cra); Lisa Werner (br). **Getty Images:** Joey Foley (cl). **8-9 Alamy Stock Photo:** US Navy Photo. **10 Alamy Stock Photo:** Israel Talby / Israel images (b). **11 Getty Images:** Apic / Hulton Archive. **12-13 Getty Images:** Fred Morley / Hulton Archive (b). **14-15 iStockphoto.com:** ElenaMirage (b). **15 Getty Images:** Sam Panthaky / AFP (t). **16 Library of Congress, Washington, D.C.:** Charles T. Webber (t). **17 Library of Congress, Washington, D.C.:** Harvey B. Lindsley (bc). **18 Alamy Stock Photo:** US Coast Guard Photo (br). **Getty Images:** Joseph Barrak / AFP (cl). **19 Alamy Stock Photo:** Jochen Tack (crb). **Rex by Shutterstock:** Global Warming Images / Shutterstock (cla). **20-21 Getty Images:** Bettmann. **23 Getty Images:** Emmanuel Dunand / AFP. **24-25 Getty Images:** Agence France Presse / Hulton Archive (b). **26 Getty Images:** David Turnley / Corbis Historical. **28 Getty Images:** Arthur Schatz / The LIFE Picture Collection (t). **29 Getty Images:** Orlando Sierra / AFP (b). **30-31 Alamy Stock Photo:** Wael Hamzeh / EPA (b). **32 Alamy Stock Photo:** Everett Collection Historical. **34-35 Getty Images:** China Photos. **39 Alamy Stock Photo:** Granger Historical Picture Archive. **40-41 Getty Images:** Bettmann (t). **41 Alamy Stock Photo:** Granger Historical Picture Archive (br). **42-43 Getty Images:** The Sydney Morning Herald / Fairfax Media (b). **44 NASA:** (cb). **44-45 NASA:** A. Fujii (Background). **45 NASA:** (t, cb, cra); ESA (crb). **47 Getty Images:** PhotoQuest. **49 Getty Images:** Popperfoto. **50-51 Wellcome Images** http://creativecommons.org/licenses/by/4.0/: Iconographic Collections (b). **52 123RF.com:** Wavebreak Media Ltd. **53 123RF.com:** Oksana Tkachuk (tr). **54 Alamy Stock Photo:** Lebrecht Music and Arts Photo Library (br). **iStockphoto.com:** GeorgiosArt (cl). **55 Alamy Stock Photo:** GL Archive (cr); Photo Researchers, Inc (bl). **Getty Images:** Dea Picture Library (tl). **56 Alamy Stock Photo:** Jerome Madramootoo / ShutterQuill (cla). **Dreamstime.com:** Walter Arce (bl). **57 Getty Images:** Sean M. Haffey (tl); Art Rickerby / The LIFE Picture Collection (cb). **Alamy Stock Photo:** Jack Sullivan (ca). **Dreamstime.com:** Mary Mallucci (cla); Ognjen Stevanovic (cb)

Jacket images: *Front:* **Dreamstime.com:** Centrill t; **Getty Images:** Judith Haeusler bl; **iStockphoto.com:** leezsnow; *Back:* **123RF.com:** Andrey Kiselev tl

Front Endpapers: **123RF.com:** belchonock 0; *Back Endpapers:* **123RF.com:** belchonock 0

All other images © Dorling Kindersley
For further information see: www.dkimages.com

A WORLD OF IDEAS:
SEE ALL THERE IS TO KNOW
www.dk.com

Contents

Words in the glossary appear in **bold**.

Chapter 1
What Makes a Hero?

We all love superheroes who save the world with amazing superpowers—but real-life heroes don't have superpowers. Their power comes from their courage, concern for others, and willingness to take action.

In this book, you'll read about real-life heroes. Some heroes put their lives on the line. Others fight for a fairer world. Some heroes take the first steps into the unknown. Others find cures for deadly diseases.

Real-life heroes don't look for headlines or **glory**. They just believe in doing the right thing.

A lifeguard practices his skills during a lifesaving drill at sea.

Young Heroes

These teenagers are all heroes. They've helped to make the world a better place.

Yusra Mardini

While fleeing war in Syria, Olympic swimmer Yusra Mardini jumped out of a sinking boat and pushed it to safety. She saved all 20 people on board.

Ishwor Ghimire

Ishwor Ghimire was helping out at a children's center in Nepal when an earthquake struck. He led all 55 children to safety.

Stephen Sutton

While battling cancer, Stephen Sutton decided to raise £10,000 for the Teenage Cancer Trust. By the time he died, he had raised £3 million.

Zach Bonner

Zach Bonner raises money for needy children through the Little Red Wagon Foundation, which he founded when he was eight years old.

Angela Zhang

When she was 17, Angela Zhang won an award for her research into cancer treatments. This important research could lead to lifesaving cures.

Chapter 2
Lifesavers

On September 11, 2001, **terrorists** crashed airplanes into the World Trade Center skyscrapers in New York City. The skyscrapers collapsed. Police, firefighters, paramedics, and others rushed in to help rescue survivors.

The terrorists aimed another plane at the United States Capitol building in Washington, DC. Passengers fought back. Although the plane crashed, it did not hit the Capitol building.

Retired Fire Chief Joseph Curry at the World Trade Center rescue operation.

Those passengers gave up their lives
so thousands of others could survive.
Many people became heroes that day.
They risked their lives to save others.

War creates many heroes, not always on the battlefield. During World War II (1939–1945), the Nazis killed millions of people, including six million Jews. Many brave people risked their lives to help those in danger.

Oskar Schindler had a factory in Poland, a country that had been invaded by the Nazis. Many of the workers at the factory were Jewish. Schindler and his wife, Emilie, protected them from the Nazis.

Oskar Schindler with his factory workers in Poland.

Raoul Wallenberg gave out special Swedish passports called Schutz-passes, which provided protection from the Nazis.

Raoul Wallenberg was a Swedish diplomat working in Hungary, another country invaded by the Nazis. He gave Jews safe places to live and issued special passes to give them protection. He saved about 100,000 people.

When the Nazis invaded Poland, Irena Sendler was working with children in the Polish city of Warsaw. Secretly, she helped about 2,000 Jewish children escape from the Nazis.

Kindertransport children arrive in Great Britain.

A British man named Nicholas Winton rescued hundreds of children from the Nazis. He sent the children to safety in Great Britain through a rescue program called Kindertransport.

Without these brave heroes, many more lives might have been lost.

Toward the end of World War II, Canadian Joan Bamford Fletcher was a nurse on the island of Sumatra in Indonesia. She led 2,000 Dutch prisoners and 70 Japanese soldiers through 500 miles (805 km) of dangerous jungles to safety.

Lifesavers work during peacetime, too. Mother Teresa devoted her life to caring for the "poorest of the poor" in Kolkata, India.

Jungle of Sumatra

The Missionaries of Charity, founded by Mother Teresa, has been helping people for more than 65 years.

She founded the Missionaries of Charity, which carries on her work around the world. Mother Teresa was made a Catholic saint in 2016.

This painting shows escaped slaves being led to safety on the Underground Railroad.

Chas T. Webber

The Underground Railroad

Harriet Tubman was a hero who risked her freedom to help others be free. She escaped slavery in the American south by traveling along a route of secret houses where slaves could hide. This secret route from the slave-owning states in the south to the free states in the north was called the Underground Railroad.

Once free, Tubman returned south time and again to lead hundreds of slaves to freedom along the Underground Railroad. With each trip, she risked being captured and made a slave again. She carried on anyway, helping others to gain their freedom.

Harriet Tubman

Heroes Together

These international organizations are made up of groups of heroes who work together to save lives.

UNICEF

The United Nations Children's Fund helps children around the world with food, shelter, health care, and education.

Coast Guard and lifeboat services

Coast Guard and lifeboat services rescue people from the seas and oceans of the world.

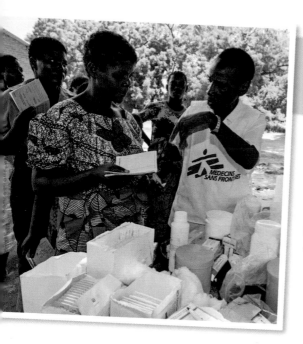

Doctors Without Borders

Also known by its French name, Médecins Sans Frontières, these doctors and nurses give medical help wherever it is needed.

International Red Cross and Red Crescent

The Red Cross and Red Crescent assist victims of natural disasters, war, and other international emergencies.

Chapter 3
Human Rights Heroes

Sometimes, it's what a hero says that changes the world. These heroes fight to make sure everyone's rights are protected.

For more than 200 years, Great Britain ruled India, but many Indians wanted their country to be independent. Mahatma Gandhi led the fight for independence. He showed the people how to **protest** without using violence. In 1947, India finally became independent. Gandhi's example of peaceful protests made him a hero.

Mahatma Gandhi leads a 240-mile (385-km) march in India in 1930.

In the country of Myanmar, also known as Burma, Aung San Suu Kyi (pronounced Ahng-Sahn-Soo-Chee) called for a fair government elected by the people. The country's military leaders put her under house arrest, which meant she was a prisoner in her own home.

For more than 25 years, she followed Mahatma Gandhi's example of peaceful protests. Finally, open elections were held in 2015, and the people of Myanmar were able to vote for their own government.

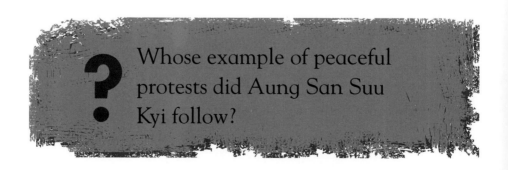

? Whose example of peaceful protests did Aung San Suu Kyi follow?

Aung San Suu Kyi speaks at a press conference of the National League for Democracy party in Myanmar.

Gandhi's example of peaceful protests also influenced Dr. Martin Luther King Jr. King spoke out to help African Americans gain fair and equal rights in the United States. He led marches and gave speeches that inspired millions.

His "I Have a Dream" speech is world famous. King said that he had a dream that one day, people of all colors and backgrounds would be treated equally.

Martin Luther King Jr. at the Freedom March in Washington, DC, USA, in 1963, where he gave his historic "I Have a Dream" speech.

His message of peace and friendship among all people continues to have powerful meaning today.

In 1948, South Africa passed laws called "apartheid." White people ran the country, while black South Africans and people of mixed race were second-class citizens. People around the world protested.

Nelson Mandela was arrested while leading the fight against apartheid. During his 27 years in prison, he was a heroic symbol of the protests. After his release, he worked with South African politicians to finally end the apartheid laws. In 1994, Mandela was elected president of his country.

South Africans campaign for Nelson Mandela in 1994.

Cesar Chavez with grape pickers at a vineyard in California, USA.

In the United States, Cesar Chavez helped farm workers to win fair pay and safer working conditions. He organized the farm workers into a **labor union** so they could work together to make things better.

Rigoberta Menchu works for the rights of **native** Mayan people in the country of Guatemala. She also protested against the civil war there. Although her work is sometimes dangerous, Menchu continues to **campaign** for the rights of people in Guatemala.

Rigoberta Menchu marches with her supporters.

In Pakistan, a group of terrorists called the Taliban did not think that girls should go to school. One brave girl, Malala Yousafzai, studied hard and spoke up for other girls who also wanted to learn. She got a lot of attention for her work.

When she was 15, a Taliban gunman shot her. Yousafzai recovered. She continues to help girls have the chance for an education. Malala Yousafzai is a young girl who became an international hero by fighting for her rights and the rights of others.

Malala Yousafzai at the opening of the Malala Yousafzai All-Girls School in Lebanon in July 2015.

The Universal Declaration of Human Rights

Eleanor Roosevelt inspired The Universal Declaration of Human Rights after World War II.

This document spells out how all people should be treated. These are some of the rights in the declaration. Sadly, many people around the world still do not have these rights.

All human beings are born free and equal.

Everyone has the right to life, liberty, and security.

Everyone has the right to freedom of thought, **conscience**, and religion.

Everyone has the right to education.

Chapter 4
Explorers!

Parade in front of the model of Zheng He's treasure ship in Nanjing, China.

The world's great explorers are heroes who put aside their fear of the unknown to seek out new places.

In the 1400s, much of the world was unexplored. Zheng He, a ship's captain from China, sailed around the Pacific and Indian Oceans. His fleet of ships even reached the southern tip of Africa.

In the 1700s, Captain James Cook of Great Britain sailed around the entire world twice, across the Atlantic, Pacific, and Indian Oceans. His explorations led to the founding of Australia and New Zealand.

In 1804, Captains Meriwether Lewis and William Clark set off on an **expedition** to explore new lands in the United States. An American Indian woman named Sacagawea helped them. Every day, they faced new challenges.

This map shows the trail of Lewis and Clark's expedition team across the United States to the Pacific Ocean—a distance of more than 3,700 miles (6,000 km). Then they had to travel back again!

Fort Clatsop

FINISH
November 1805

Location in the United States

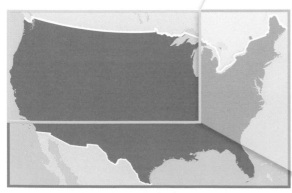

They sailed down swiftly flowing rivers and crossed tall mountains. They found new kinds of animals and plants. They met many American Indians. Lewis and Clark kept journals on their expedition. Later, people used these journals as a guide to explore the western United States.

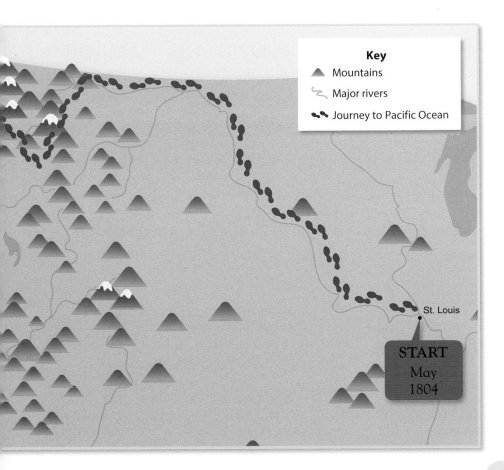

Key

▲ Mountains

〜 Major rivers

•• Journey to Pacific Ocean

St. Louis

START
May
1804

In 1903, brothers Orville and Wilbur Wright invented the first working airplane. They bravely took to the sky, not knowing if their plane would ever take flight. Their first successful flight lasted 12 seconds. Thanks to the Wright brothers, air travel is now common.

More pilots began to explore the air. In 1932, Amelia Earhart was the first woman pilot to fly across the Atlantic Ocean on her own. She also flew across the United States and back again. Sadly, her plane disappeared on a flight across the Pacific Ocean. However, Earhart's adventurous flights paved the way for other pilots.

? When was the first working airplane invented?

American pilot Amelia Earhart

Ernest Shackleton's ship, *Endurance*, trapped in ice.

In 1914, British explorer Ernest Shackleton set off to explore Antarctica. His ship, the *Endurance*, got trapped in ice! He and his crew were stuck for more than a year. Shackleton led a small team across the Antarctic to find help. He saved his entire crew and became a hero.

Edmund Hillary from Great Britain and Tenzing Norgay of Nepal became heroes when they climbed the highest mountain in the world—Mount Everest.

Hillary and Norgay were the first to climb Mount Everest. Since then, hundreds of other adventurers have followed in their footsteps.

Edmund Hillary and Tenzing Norgay near the top of Mount Everest in May 1953.

French explorer Jacques Cousteau wanted to dive deep under the ocean where no one had been before. In 1943, he invented scuba diving, with equipment that allows divers to breathe underwater. Cousteau became famous for his underwater films.

Sylvia Earle is an American marine biologist who dives deep beneath the ocean's surface to study plants and animals. Earle leads a campaign to protect the world's oceans.

Canadian movie director James Cameron became fascinated by deep sea diving while filming the movie, *Titanic*. He was the first solo diver to explore the bottom of the Mariana Trench, the deepest point on Earth. It is nearly seven miles (11 km) deep.

Sylvia Earle dives underwater to observe a shark.

Space Explorers

The space explorers who first soared out of the Earth's atmosphere were heroes, too.

Yuri Gagarin from the Soviet Union (now Russia) became the first human in space when he orbited Earth in 1961.

American astronauts Neil Armstrong and Edwin "Buzz" Aldrin became the first humans to set foot on the Moon in 1969.

Since 1998, space explorers from around the world have taken turns to live and work on board the International Space Station.

Chapter 5
Heroes of Medicine

The fight against deadly diseases needs heroes, too. **Vaccines** protect people from getting certain diseases. In 1796, British doctor Edward Jenner invented the first vaccine. It prevented smallpox, a dangerous disease that had no cure. Now there are vaccines to prevent many different diseases.

In 1952, American doctor Jonas Salk developed a vaccine to prevent polio, a muscle disease that affected millions of people, especially children. Salk's vaccine means that today, the world is nearly rid of polio.

Jonas Salk saved many lives with the polio vaccine.

In 1863, French scientist Louis Pasteur discovered a way to kill **bacteria** so that food stays safe and healthy longer. His process is called "pasteurization." Pasteur also developed vaccines for the deadly diseases of rabies and anthrax.

An antibiotic is a medicine used to kill bacteria that cause infection. Scottish doctor Alexander Fleming discovered the first antibiotic in 1928. He was growing mold in a dish and noticed that it killed the surrounding bacteria. He called it penicillin. The work of Fleming and others made penicillin an important lifesaver.

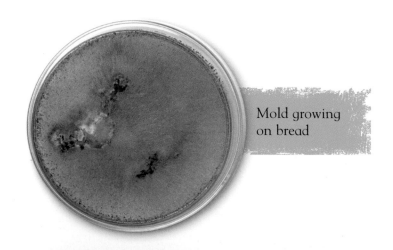

Mold growing on bread

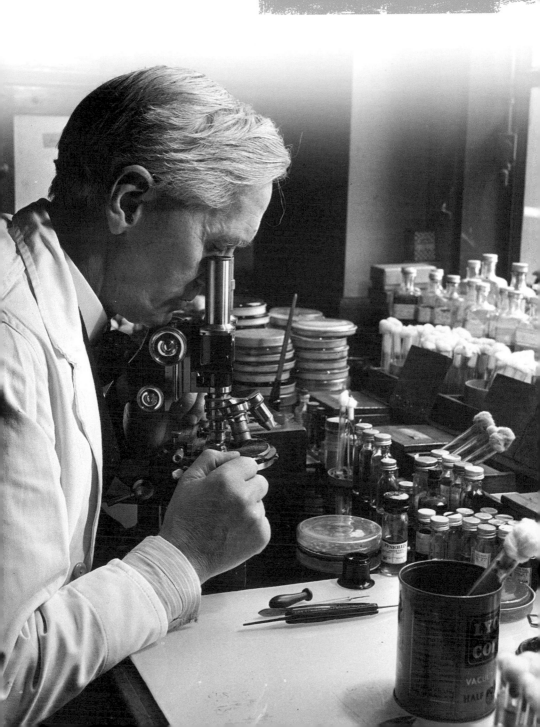

Alexander Fleming looks through a microscope at his laboratory in London, England.

Florence Nightingale was a British nurse who saved the lives of many soldiers during the Crimean War (1854–1856). Nightingale saw soldiers dying of infections in dirty hospitals. She showed that patients are more likely to survive in clean hospitals. Nightingale founded modern nursing. Since then, nurses have helped to save millions of people!

Florence Nightingale at a hospital in Scutari, Turkey during the Crimean War.

Mary Seacole of Jamaica used her savings to travel to the Crimea to care for the soldiers. She set up a hospital there and risked her life to help soldiers on the battlefields.

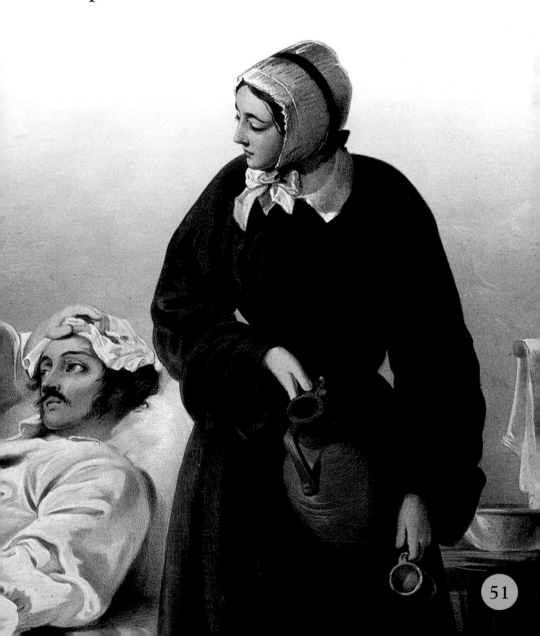

Millions of lives are saved every day by giving blood **transfusions** to sick or injured patients. In the 1930s, an African-American doctor named Charles Drew made blood transfusions possible by developing a way to **preserve** blood for longer.

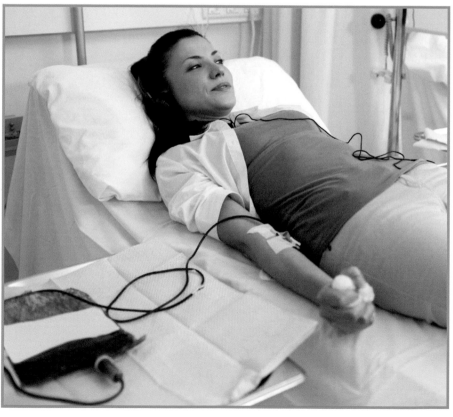

Woman donating blood for transfusions.

This means that the blood given by donors can be stored safely until it is needed. This blood can then be put into the patient who needs it.

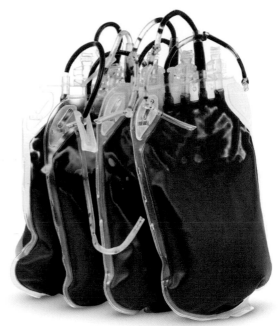

Donors' blood is stored in special bags.

Blood donors give some of their blood to save other people's lives. They're heroes, too!

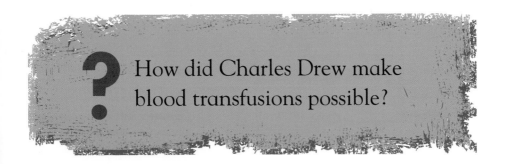

? How did Charles Drew make blood transfusions possible?

Heroes of Science

These heroes of science had **groundbreaking** ideas that changed the way we think about the world.

Isaac Newton

Newton first explained how gravity works by using the example of an apple falling from a tree.

Marie Curie and Irena Joliot-Curie

These mother and daughter scientists researched radioactive chemicals, which led to lifesaving treatments.

Charles Darwin

Darwin's study of nature led to the **theory** of evolution, which states that humans are related to apes.

Albert Einstein

Einstein's theories of relativity involving energy, matter, and time, changed the study of physics.

Rachel Carson

Carson was a nature writer who first warned of the dangers of damaging the environment.

Sports Heroes

These sports heroes are record-breakers who have inspired the world.

Usain Bolt
Sprinter Usain Bolt won gold in the 100-meter and 200-meter races, and the sprint relay at three Olympic Games. His achievement is known as the "triple triple!"

Serena Williams
Since becoming professional at age 14, tennis star Serena Williams has won more than 90 tournaments, including doubles with her sister, Venus.

Turia Pitt

Despite having severe burns over most of her body, Turia Pitt competes in Ironman triathlons, swimming 2.4 miles (3.8 km), cycling 112 miles (180 km) and running 26.2 miles (42 km).

Pelé

Soccer superstar Pelé led the Brazil team to three World Cup victories. Pelé has used his fame to help children around the world.

Awards

These are some awards given to people for heroic deeds.

Congressional Medal of Honor, *USA*

Légion d'Honneur, *France*

Victoria Cross, *Great Britain*

Nobel Prize, *worldwide*

Real-Life Heroes Quiz

Find the answers to these questions about what you have read.

1 Who protected Jewish workers from the Nazis at his factory during World War II?

2 Who risked capture to lead hundreds of slaves to freedom on the Underground Railroad?

3 Who had a dream that one day, people of all colors and backgrounds would be treated equally?

4 Who invented the first working airplane?

5 Who was the first human in space?

6 Which two nurses cared for soldiers during the Crimean War?

Answers on page 61.

Glossary

bacteria
tiny living things. Some bacteria cause diseases

campaign
take a series of actions toward a particular goal

conscience
personal beliefs and morals

expedition
journey to explore

glory
receiving praise and honor

groundbreaking
opening the way for new possibilities

labor union
organization of workers who campaign for better wages and working conditions

native
originally from a certain place

preserve

keep free from decay

protest

taking action to bring about change

terrorists

people who use violence to justify
their goal

theory

an explanation that is widely accepted

transfusion

transfer of blood from donor into
the bloodstream of another

vaccines

treatment that makes the body stronger
against infections

Answers to the Real-life Heroes Quiz:

1. Oskar Schindler **2.** Harriet Tubman **3.** Martin Luther
King Jr. **4.** Orville and Wilbur Wright **5.** Yuri Gagarin
6. Florence Nightingale and Mary Seacole

Guide for Parents

DK Readers is a four-level interactive reading adventure series for children, developing the habit of reading widely for both pleasure and information. These books have an exciting main narrative interspersed with a range of reading genres to suit your child's reading ability. Each book is designed to develop your child's reading skills, fluency, grammar awareness, and comprehension in order to build confidence and engagement when reading.

Ready for a *Beginning to Read Alone* book

YOUR CHILD SHOULD

- be able to read many words without needing to stop and break them down into sound parts.
- read smoothly, in phrases and with expression.
  By this level, your child will be beginning to read silently.
- self-correct when a word or sentence doesn't sound right.

A VALUABLE AND SHARED READING EXPERIENCE

For some children, text reading, particularly nonfiction, requires much effort, but adult participation can make this both fun and easier. So here are a few tips on how to use this book with your child.

TIP 1 Check out the contents together before your child begins:

- invite your child to check the blurb, contents page, and layout of the book and comment on it.
- ask your child to make predictions about the story.
- talk about the information your child might want to find out.

TIP 2 Encourage fluent and flexible reading:

- support your child to read in fluent, expressive phrases, making full use of punctuation and thinking about the meaning.
- help your child learn to read with expression by choosing a sentence to read aloud and demonstrating how to do this.

TIP 3 Indicators that your child is reading for meaning:

- your child will be responding to the text if he/she is self-correcting and varying his/her voice.
- your child will want to talk about what he/she is reading or is eager to turn the page to find out what will happen next.

TIP 4 Chat at the end of each chapter:

- encourage your child to recall specific details after each chapter.
- let your child pick out interesting words and discuss what they mean.
- talk about what each of you found most interesting or most important.
- ask questions about the text. These help to develop comprehension skills and awareness of the language used.

A FEW ADDITIONAL TIPS

- Read to your child regularly to demonstrate fluency, phrasing, and expression; to find out or check information; and for sharing enjoyment.
- Encourage your child to reread favorite texts to increase reading confidence and fluency.
- Check that your child is reading a range of different types of material, such as poems, jokes, and following instructions.

Series consultant, **Dr. Linda Gambrell**, Distinguished Professor of Education at Clemson University, has served as President of the National Reading Conference, the College Reading Association, and the International Reading Association.

Index